I0162865

Cover design
by Rita Toews

Photography
Jeffrey Crimmel

Every day domesticated animals are born on the streets
where they live. Some are born in developed countries
like the U.S. and Canada while others begin their lives
in third world countries like Mexico. Most of these
street animals do not live long in the harsh conditions
in a world without human care. Some are lucky and
escape the life on the streets. Here is a story of
Centavo, a dog from Mexico, who was fortunate to
survive and enjoy a full life with a family of humans
who adopted her and made a difference.

Centavo

A Dog From Mexico

Jeffrey R Crimmel

4

Acknowledgments

In Memory of Steve Forman

About the Author

Photos

Dictionario

Chapter 1
Centavo
The Early Years

The first thing Centavo remembered was that she was a dog. Being a dog was one thing but being born a dog in a country called Mexico without a home was another. Centavo had two puppy brothers and one puppy sister she competed with for milk. Her mother, Cha Cha, gave birth to her family near a beach by a small fishing village on the Sea of Cortez. Being near the beach was a good place for dogs without a home, because many people came to the sandy areas near the water to eat food and drink different kinds of liquid. They did not always eat everything they brought with them. Many times Cha Cha could find food thrown away in the trash cans near the beach. The more food she found the more milk she could produce to feed Centavo and her puppy brothers and sister.

Being a dog is not always what it is cracked up to be. There is an expression used in the human world. When someone says to another human, "You are living a dog's life", the words are meant to describe that person as having an easy life just like a dog. All they need to do was wake up, eat, have walks, bark and sleep. This expression seemed to be about the dogs living in a country to the north of Mexico called the United States. The description did not seem to match Centavo and other dogs born on the streets in Mexico.

When Centavo was one month old her sister died because she could not get enough milk to drink from her mother. Cha Cha did her best to care for the four puppies but she could not always get food to eat in the cold period called winter because no humans would come to the beach to be on the sand and swim in the water. If no people came to the ocean then there was no food thrown away and nothing for Cha Cha to eat. A kind human found the young puppy and dug a hole and buried Centavo's sister before the rats and other animals that ate dead things found her body.

Life in Mexico was not easy for a dog, especially the ones who did not have a human to care for them and give them food. Cha Cha never had a human as an owner. She had to learn how to survive by finding the places where old food was thrown away and where kind people lived that sometimes gave her scraps of meat fat or cheese rinds. As Centavo got older she learned from her mother where to go and find things to eat. Because the family lived near the ocean they could sleep, curled up near the cement wall that was found along the beach and stay out of the wind. They did not have to go into town to find a place to sleep. Not everyone was kind to Cha Cha and her family because they did not have a human family and no one wanted dogs around that did not have an owner. Cha Cha would tell her puppies to run when young boys or men started throwing rocks at them. This meant they were not wanted and leaving was the best option.

When Centavo was six or seven months old she had to start looking out for herself. Her mother, Cha Cha, was going to have more puppies. The big black dog that came through the beach area where they lived and looked like a wolf was the father.

Black dog from down the beach

Centavo did not know who her father was but she did know the big black dog down the beach was not related to her. Centavo was long in length and short in height with thick hair, which helped keep her warm in the winter. She once heard a human say,

"Look, that dog looks like one of the dogs the Queen of England owns."

Centavo did not know who the Queen of England was so she had no idea what this human was talking about. The human also spoke a different language than the people who live in the small town near the beach. Centavo was a smart dog and, using her good dog thinking, she figured out the person who made the comment about her looking like a dog owned by a Queen must be from another land where they still had Queens. She knew there were no Queens living in the village near the beach because Pero, the wisest dog living on the streets, would know about it.

Pero was a male dog Cha Cha introduced to her remaining children when they started living on their own. She knew if her young daughter and sons knew Pero and needed to ask him something, he would find them an answer. Pero was a short dog, a little taller than Centavo with the same color hair as her. Most dogs were taller than Centavo and this sometimes was an advantage when tourists came to town.

Cha Cha

"Look John. There is a cute short dog living at the beach all by itself. Do we have any scraps we can feed it? Maybe if it got more to eat it would grow taller?"

Centavo never grew taller but she was able to get more scraps than the tall dogs roaming the beach. Centavo thought she looked a lot like Pero and she guessed maybe the reason her mother had introduced her to him had something to do with the possibility he was her father. Centavo was also smart like Pero and in Mexico that is an important thing to be, especially if you are a dog. There is an expression in this country that states,

"There are only smart dogs in Mexico."

Centavo thought this comment referred to the fact that, in order to survive in this country and you are a dog without a home, you have to learn quickly and use all your talents to get your next meal. Learning to cross the street and watch out for the cars driving down the road was a lesson that needed to be learned at a young age. Some puppies and young dogs did not learn the art of crossing the road and they never returned to the beach again. There were many dogs like Centavo born on the streets without a home. These dogs must use the knowledge they either learned from their mothers or from watching other dogs trying to survive on the streets.

Pero, the wise street dog

Chapter 2

Growing Up

Centavo was now a year old. Because she was a female, many of the male dogs on the streets started to pay a lot of attention to her at certain times. Her mother told her to be careful of those dogs. Cha Cha wanted a better life for Centavo so she gave her daughter advice whenever they crossed paths.

"Raising puppies all the time is a lot of work and responsibility Centavo. You do not need such a burden at a young age."

Because of her shortness, Centavo had an advantage in escaping the attentions of male dogs. She knew where a low fence was located that only she could go under. On the other side was a small alley. The fence was put up to block the young boys from riding their bikes through the alley and making a lot of noise. The older man who put up the barrier wanted peace and quiet in his retirement years and stopping the bike riders from coming down his alley was a way to help secure that goal. The fence worked out well for Centavo when 'Grrrr' or 'leave me alone' didn't work.

Fishermen who live in the village work a lot on their boats and fishing nets on the beach where Centavo lived. They fish for different kinds of seafood at different times of the year. In September the season for catching a small type of sea animal called a shrimp or camaron begins. Small boats called pangas would go out on the Sea of Cortez and the fishermen would toss their nets and wait for the little gray animals to get caught in the web. They then pull them into the boat.

The Shrimp Festival, held every year in the town, happens in November. Many tourists come across the border to celebrate in the eating and drinking of liquids that made the humans act funny. This was a good time for dogs without homes because the trashcans were always full of partially eaten meals on paper plates. Lots of beans, rice and sometimes some unfinished shrimp filled the cans. Centavo was too short to get up and into the containers overflowing with leftover food. She had to wait for a plate to fall off the top of the trash pile or team up with one of the larger dogs. The big dogs would jump up on their hind legs and pull a few plates down to the ground. Centavo usually was allowed to share what the larger dog was able to bring to the ground because she stood watch for the police and military humans who chased dogs like her and her companions away with sticks. She would give a warning bark if a uniformed human approached and the pack of stray dogs, including Centavo, would make their escape, hopefully with full stomachs. The stray dogs wished the Shrimp Festival happened every weekend so they could eat well for at least a few days.

Mexican dancers at the Shrimp Festival

Other events happened in this small town near the ocean that bring many people who speak a different language. Centavo learned the name of the village were she lived was called San Felipe. She was told this from Pero during the last festival. Centavo also found out from Pero the language, spoken by the foreign visitors, was called English. Right now all she knew was they used different words for different things. Leche was called 'milk'

and they called carne 'meat' in their language.
Some of these foreigners tried to speak the
language of the town people and Centavo thought
this was a good thing. At least they were trying to
be a part of the Mexican culture and learning the
language of the people in San Felipe was a good
start.

Racing funny cars in the desert was one of the other
events that happened in town. Centavo never saw
the cars race because she lived on the beach but
before the event she got to watch the vehicles
parade down the main street along the ocean called
the Malecon. These cars were different than the
regular cars the humans drove. Some looked like
they had cages over the top of the wheels and the
drivers had to use plastic covers over their eyes to
keep out the dirt and sand that flew up when they
raced.

Pero used to be owned by a human family. He was
once taken to such a race outside of town. He told
Centavo all about the noisy cars when they took off
and leaped into the air while going over bumps. He
also said these crazy races happened several times a
year and it was one of the main reasons the
foreigners from the north came to their small town.

The people of San Felipe seem to like the special holidays because a lot of the tourist items are sold at this time. Pottery, funny tee shirts, hats and jewelry are just a few of the many items the foreigners purchase. Food and drink of Mexico also seemsdd to be a favorite pastime for tourists to indulge in. Centavo could see these people, who spoke a different language, were always dressed well and had plenty of paper in a leather container used to carry something called dollars. They called their paper 'dollars' and the Mexican people called their paper 'pesos.' They both seemed to do the same job of getting stuff in return such as food and gifts in the tourist shops. The foreign money was accepted in all the stores.

Chapter 3

Tough Times

Centavo was now almost two years old. She had been surviving on the beach her entire life and she knew no other way to live. Her mother, Cha Cha was raising another family of puppies and this time the father was a brown dog who came from another town in Mexico and was left on the beach by his owners. His name was Tai and he said his owners could no longer buy food for him because the tourist in his town stopped coming and visiting Mexico.

The owners ran a restaurant that cooked food the same as in the country in the north called the Estados Unidos. Without the foreigners coming to their town, they made little money and they had to make changes. Getting rid of Tai was the first change. The owners thought Tai would have a better chance of surviving in a beach town where fish were caught instead of the busy border town where his human family came from.

Tai was also smart. Being owned by humans before becoming a street dog could have been a disadvantage but he learned quickly how to find food and which dogs to stay away from so that he did not get into fights. Fighting takes a lot of energy. Staying away from problems with other dogs was the best solution. Fighting meant having to find even more food l because the energy of living things comes from food and fighting takes a lot of energy. He was not afraid of the other dogs on the street; He just did not see the point of getting bitten and having to heal from such encounters over a left over pizza slice when he could move on to the next trash can and maybe find a bone or a spare rib.

Tai getting warm in the sun

Chapter 4

Centavo Finds a Home

Sometimes good things in life happen without any explanation. If Centavo had been a Buddhist or Hindu in a previous life, what was about happen must have had something to do with her good deeds in that life. This was called Karma. In the western religions, living a good life was a way to get into heaven. Whatever religious influence one may follow does not matter in this case. Centavo's life was about to change dramatically.

After eating some fish the week before, Centavo swallowed some netting used to catch the fish. It was wrapped around the meal and since dogs do not have thumbs and fingers needed to remove the unwanted fishing material, everything was eaten. The plastic net did not digest well in the stomach of Centavo and she did not feel good at all. She hoped she was not getting sick because a sick dog living on the streets usually died. Usually there was no human to care for them and give them medicine to cure the illness.

Just when she was about to go to Pero and ask him what to do, she noticed two human tourists offering her food. Centavo did not feel real hungry because the plastic in her stomach interfered with her feeling good. At the same time it was not every day a human offered a stray dog food and she walked over to the couple and took the beef from the taco they were offering and ate it. She did not know when her next meal would come and she knew had to eat in order to survive.

The man and woman were talking about Centavo. By now she could understand a lot of the language the humans from the north used to speak because so many of them came to San Felipe to either fish, relax, enjoy the food or just shop for tourist items to bring back to their country as gifts. Centavo heard the word 'rescue' several times. The woman was talking to the Mexicans near the beach asking if anyone owned the short dog and she pointed to Centavo. The woman spoke in the language of the humans in Mexico so Centavo knew she must be smart in order to speak two languages.

Centavo did not run away because the man tourist kept rubbing her. She like the feel of his fingers and hands on her neck and back. Having never been touched by people before, this became a new experience. She liked it. Centavo found out later the humans called this 'petting' in English or

'besuqueo' in Spanish and it is done a lot by those who own dogs. By now the woman finished asking the local fishermen and vendors if anyone own Centavo. They all said no one owned her. Every Mexican she asked, who lived near the Malecon, also told the Senora the short brown dog had lived on the waterfront all its' life and looked for food wherever she could in order to survive. They also told her there were many dogs like Centavo living on the streets and having someone give one of the dogs a home would be a good thing.

The man and woman from Estados Unidos were engaged in serious discussion and speaking too fast for Centavo to understand all they were talking about. She liked them and they kept giving her more beef from the tacos they were eating. The next thing Centavo realized was the couple were talking to her. They were saying things like,

"How would you like to come live with us? Do you think you would like it? You would get food every day."

Centavo did not know the answer to the first two questions at all. She had no idea what living with them meant or if she would like it. She only knew her life on the streets in the fishing village where she was born. She did like the third thing they said, something about food every day. Since she was a street dog, food was a high priority. Centavo was smart and she barked her approval.

The couple kept petting her. The woman went to one of the vendors and purchased a collar and put it around Centavo. Centavo understood what this meant because she had seen other dogs owned by humans in the village wearing this leather thing around their necks. The woman also purchased a long leather string and attached it to the collar around her neck. This made Centavo a little nervous because she had never had these things happen to her before. She always went where she wanted to without humans directing her movements. Because she was a dog, Centavo had a special sense when humans were being kind or being mean. She could sense they were good and gentle people and she trusted them as they took her to their car.

Centavo had never ridden in a car before. She was too short to jump into the car by herself so the man picked her up and lifted her into the back seat. The humans had made a bed of towels for her to sleep on. Centavo was surrounded by suitcases on both sides of her soft resting spot in the car. The soft material felt good to Centavo. Because she did not feel well, and the warm soft bed felt so good,

Centavo fell asleep soon after the car started and moved down the road.

The journey in the car took a long time. There were several stops along the way including a military checkpoint and another crossing that took a long time. The first stop was only a quick check of the car by a human in a brown uniform. He was looking for something but Centavo did not know what it was because he never found it. He made a comment to the couple driving the car when he saw Centavo in the back seat.

"Es su pero?" he asked.

The woman who spoke both languages answered,

"Si, pero es nuestros."

Centavo understood the Spanish and now realized she was owned by a human. She was not completely awake and felt sleepy because she still did not feel good. Also when the car moved it helped her fall back to sleep at once. The humans made one stop on the road to feed themselves and let Centavo out of the car to also eat, drink and use the side of the road to relieve herself. They attached the long leather string to her collar before letting her out of the car. They did not want their new dog to run away because she was frightened. Centavo still did not feel good and had no intention of running away. These humans were feeding her, giving her water and allowing her to irrigate the plants on the side of the road. She had never used the bushes before while attached to a leather string but Centavo did not care at the moment. She was sure she would adjust to the lack of privacy. She was now a dog who was owned by a human.

The second stop took a long time. The humans drove into a line filled with other cars that slowly moved towards a large barrier, which had many openings for the vehicles to pass through. Centavo was awake by now and could observe more of the activity happening outside the back window where she sat. While the car crept slowly along the lane with the other cars, many Mexican humans came up to the drivers and offered things to sell. There were window shades, candy, drinks, music disks, crafts made in Mexico and hats or sombreros. No one in Mexico wore these large shade hats any more except for the Mariachi men who wore old style costumes and played songs like 'La Cucaracha' for the tourists. The gringos still liked the sombreros and would walk around the village of San Felipe with a bottle in one hand and a sombrero on their head and pretend to be a Mexican. Even a dog knew they looked stupid and Centavo also knew the drink with the XX on the bottle made tourists do crazy things.

The humans did not purchase any items sold while they slowly drove towards the great barrier in the road. They did pay for a service, which many men and young boys were offering. These vendors would wash the cars as they moved. They carried water bottles and a stick with rubber on it to wipe the windows of the cars after it was sprayed with liquid. They also had cloth rags to wipe down the car and remove the dust from the road during the long trip to the great barrier. For a few coins the car would be cleaned. Centavo was about to enter the country to the north in a shiny car with two humans who now said they owned her. Centavo knew nothing about Karma but at this moment she started to realize things in her life were about to change a lot.

The person at the great barrier also had on a uniform and spoke the language of her owners. The humans handed the man in the dark clothing a couple of small books. He asked the man driving the car,

"Is that your dog?"

Centavo thought this was a stupid question. Of course she was their dog. She wore a collar. The couple fed her. They rubbed her back all the time. She was lying on a bed in the back seat of their car. Whose dog would she be? Centavo had little patience for silly human questions that even a dog could answer.

After the man answered 'yes' to the question, the human in the uniform asked them.

"Where are you going?"

"Flagstaff, Arizona" was their reply

"Doesn't it get cold in Flagstaff?" asked the guard.

"Yes, in the winter we even have snow."

Centavo knew the English word 'cold' but not this new word, 'snow'. She was glad her fur was thick because she could tolerate cold and had done so for two years living at the beach in San Felipe.

The human at the great barrier told her new owners to,

"Have a good trip."

Centavo went back to sleep and woke up when the car stopped again at another place called Dateland. The humans again needed to eat some food and give Centavo something to eat and drink as well. This time a can of dog food was purchased, opened and put on a paper plate. Centavo smelled it and

decided it was okay to eat and did so in three big
bites. The softness of the meal in a can made
eating easy. There were no bones in it like the fish
she ate on the beach in Mexico and the smell was
almost like food that was fresh. It was like nothing
she had ever eaten before. Even the water tasted
different in this new country.

The humans ate something called a sandwich and
the male human drank a drink called a date shake.
He seemed to enjoy the drink and made lots of
funny noises as he sucked the liquid through the
straw. While he was drinking the cold shake he
took Centavo over to a grass area near the forest of
trees that grew the fruit called dates used in the
shake he was drinking. Centavo needed to relieve
herself again and this time she did more than just
water a plant. The strangest thing happened after
Centavo finished relieving herself, which was
something she never witnessed living in Mexico.
The man had a plastic bag with him and when
Centavo was finished he scooped up the 'poop' into
the bag and put it in the trash or 'basura'

Centavo thought about all the times she had
relieved her self and never had anyone pick it up
and put it into a can. She also thought about all the
other stray dogs living in her home village. They
never had any humans clean up after them. This
country called the United States was already

becoming a different place than anything Centavo had ever experienced. Soft food in a can with no bones, sweet tasting water, and humans who cleaned up a dog's 'poop' with a plastic bag and put it into a can. Centavo knew she was 'not in Mexico anymore.'

By now Centavo had figured out the name of the male driver because the woman kept calling him Scott. She called him other names as well such as 'sweetie' or 'honey' but Scott was the word she used most of the time when she was talking to him. He in turn used the word Pam mostly when he spoke to her as well as all those other words having something to do with candy. Centavo now knew the names of the two humans who picked her up at the beach in Mexico and gave her a home. Centavo still did not know what the home was like because they were still driving in a car in order to get to this town called Flagstaff. The adventure was just beginning for Centavo, the dog from Mexico.

Chapter 5

Flagstaff

Most of the drive went through desert countryside, which contained similar vegetation and plants as the desert near Centavo's hometown. Large green cactuses and the trees with thorns grew everywhere. One small community along the way, with the name Gila Bend, even had a building with a strange round object on top of it. Centavo could not read the words on signs but she heard Scott call the round object a space ship. The structure was built to attract other humans to eat in the restaurant and stay in the rooms overnight. There were many strange things Centavo had never seen in her short life and the space ship hotel was one of them.

After an hour of driving Centavo could see more cars on the road than she knew existed. Also buildings appeared, which were taller than any of the hotels along the beach in San Felipe. The roads were called highways and they contained many lanes for all the cars driving down them. They were approaching a city called Phoenix because she heard Pam mention the name. This was an area of the country where many humans must like to live because there were so many of them hurrying everywhere in their cars and trucks. Centavo was feeling overwhelmed. For a dog living on the streets of a small Mexican village only hours before, the change was somewhat frightening.

Pam and Scott made one more stop for another sandwich in a small community outside the big city. This community was called Anthem and many shoppers seemed to come from the big city just to shop in the stores found in this town. Pam said something about good prices for items sold to the other humans. She seemed to know a lot about shopping. Scott did all the driving and again made sure Centavo had enough to drink. He even found a place with bushes so Centavo could water them. A plastic bag was in his hand just in case another cleanup was needed but nothing happened at this time.

Centavo got a good look around the parking lot and street where the car was parked. None of the roads had holes in them. All the cement along the sides of the stores and roads were in place without any damage to it. The stores were painted and looked like new. The biggest change for Centavo was the lack of overflowing trashcans like in her beach town. All the dogs wore collars and were attached to a leather string like she was when Scott walked her around the stores. There were no stray dogs

without owners and that was probably a good thing because there was nothing for them to eat.
Every store and building was clean and in spotless condition.

They were soon driving up the road again but this time the car seemed to be going uphill. The plants outside the window were changing and soon the large cactus could no longer be found. In their place small bushes appeared and tall hills surrounded the car as it continued on the upward journey. Centavo had seen similar mountains before because there were many such high places only many miles to the west of San Felipe. Some of the hills came down to the sea near the fishing community but none of the other street dogs had ever explored the area just to the north of her town.

Centavo was now riding in a car and going through these mountains. Few humans lived along the road and no tall buildings could be seen anywhere. Soon the vegetation changed into something never seen by Centavo and probably never by any dog from her village. Trees growing up to the sky started to appear next to the road. The number of these giant plants was so many, Centavo could not see more than a few feet behind the first row of them. There were so many trees Centavo started to wonder how humans could live in this area. The air was also different and Centavo needed to take more breaths every minute. She still did not feel well but she did not want to miss seeing all the different sights outside the car window.

The trees near the road gave way to a few small towns that appeared to be built in clear areas. Bridges started to appear in greater numbers and another sight came into focus for Centavo. Far in the distance another hill, rising high into the heavens appeared, only this one had a distinct difference. On the top part of the hill was something white in color. It covered most of the top part of the hill while the lower parts were orange and yellow in many areas. The green color must have been more of the tall plants, which Centavo heard Pam call pine trees. The fall or 'otono' time of year was happening at the moment and the change was much more dramatic in the high altitude town of Flagstaff than in the desert fishing village of San Felipe.

Thirty minutes later, after seeing the tall mountain with white, orange, yellow and green covering its enormous sides, the car came into the town called Flagstaff. Centavo now knew the hills surrounding this town were called mountains because Pam kept saying,

"Mira!" Pam spoke to Centavo in Spanish sometimes. "Do you see the tall mountain? It is the biggest mountain in all of Arizona. The orange and yellow colors on the mountain are the aspen trees changing color. Esta muy bonita, si?

Centavo did think it was a beautiful mountain but she still did not feel well and could not get excited about all the wonderful sights she was seeing from the car window.

The car soon drove up a short hill into an area with many 'casas' or homes. Scott pushed a button on a small black object attached to a cover he pulled down when the sun came into the car and hurt his eyes. After pushing the button he turned off the street and towards a house with a door starting to rise, allowing the car to be parked in a protected area filled with many things humans used for building. Another car, much bigger than the one they rode in, was also parked in the building with the door that went up and down. Centavo was beyond being overwhelmed and could only sit there and trust her new family. She had no idea having someone to care for her would mean there would be so much change in her life. It was too late to go back. Mexico and her life by the sea was a long ways away.

Chapter 6

A New Home

Centavo did not know how long she slept. It could have been days for all she knew. All she was sure of was it had been the most comfortable bed and longest she had ever slept at one time. Centavo had a lot of dreams during this first night away from Mexico. She saw Pero and her mother Cha Cha during her 'sueno' or dream time and they both seemed to be giving her the same message.

"Don't worry about us. Take advantage of your good fortune and live the good life of a dog in the Estados Unidos."

Scott had carried Centavo from the car and placed her into a bed inside the house yesterday. She had only been in a house once or twice before when she lived in Mexico. It was nothing like the house of her new owners. Before she had only peeked into the Mexican houses when the door was left open, hoping to find some food. Mexican 'pisos' or floors are either made with tile or packed earth. The walls in some houses have colorful pictures and the walls are usually painted in bright colors. The new house in Flagstaff where her bed was located had some type of material covering the floor. The soft feel of the fabric covering felt better than any sand Centavo ever slept on at the beach. She remembered being laid in a bed and falling asleep almost instantly. Her head was filled with enough new images to last a lifetime.

The light coming through a large glass door woke Centavo. She had smelled another dog when she was placed into her bed but was too tired to give it much thought. Now that she was awake the dog smell was again evident and she even heard a few barks in the other room behind the closed door. Scott, her new human owner, came into the room and closed the door behind him. Centavo could hear the other dog in the next room and it sounded excited and started to bark.

"Be quiet Jackson," came the command from Pam in the next room.

Scott opened the glass door by sliding it to the side. The area behind the door had green grass growing in a large area. Scott called Centavo to come outside. She had not watered any bushes in a while and this grass area had many bushes that needed watering. Centavo also had not 'pooped' since yesterday and the new area was a private place to do so. Scott did not attach the leather string to Centavo when she went out and he left her alone as she sniffed all the plants and bushes and found the perfect place to relieve herself after the long journey to her new home.

Grass was not new to Centavo. A small square called the Glorietta in San Felipe had grass growing in the middle of it as well. One day Centavo and another street dog walked the ten blocks to the circle just to lie on their backs and wiggle. The grass was like a back scratcher and it felt good. They continued to roll on the green ground cover until a man in a brown uniform with a long stick, called a hoe, came along and chased them off. Centavo figured the grass must have been grown just to look at and not meant for street dogs to roll on and scratch their backs. Now Centavo lived in a house with its' own private area where a dog could roll over and squirm all it wanted to without the fear of being chased off by a man with a hoe. Could this place be 'dog heaven?'

After a period of time in which Centavo explored the back area, Scott called to Centavo to come inside. He asked if she was hungry. He kept saying to her,

"Do you want some food?"

'Food' was a word she had learned from the tourist on the beach in Mexico and Centavo answered with,

"Arf!' This time 'arf' meant yes. 'Arf' can mean two things to a dog and only dogs seem to know the difference between the 'arf' meaning yes and the 'arf' meaning no. It probably has something to do with where the dog places the accent on the bark.

Because the weather was still nice and Centavo seemed to be enjoying the smells of the different plants and bushes in the grass area of the house, Scott brought out a bowl of round, dry nuggets with some of the soft food without bones. Centavo smelled it and ate a couple of the balls just to make sure it was food. She had never had food that came in small round spheres before and she like the taste a lot. Within a few minutes the bowl was empty and the growl in her stomach stopped.

Pam, Centavo's bi lingual human woman owner, came outside with Scott and they started to talk rapidly in their language. Only the words, 'dog', 'meet' and 'friends' were understood. Being a smart dog from Mexico, Centavo figured the other dog in the next room was going to come out and the couple wanted the other dog to meet her. Pam hoped they would get along. Pam went back into the house and opened the door leading to more areas of the house.

Through the door bolted a ball of fur about twelve inches taller than Centavo and about the six inches longer in length. This other dog raced past Centavo and ran around the grass area four or five times, barking as it circled the lawn. The dog seemed to have the name Jackson because the owners kept saying to this excited dog,

"Jackson, stop barking," or "Jackson, calm down."

Centavo had never seen a dog with as much energy as Jackson. The only other time Centavo saw a street dog in Mexico act like this dog was when one of her brothers, Peso, found a paper cup filled with the black morning liquid humans drank. (Cha Cha named all her puppies after Mexican money.) A tourist sat on the wall near the beach eating a breakfast burrito. When he left he forgot his coffee and Peso found it. Peso was able to get his tongue into the container and drink the whole thing. For the next two hours her brother ran around 'loco' and barked so quickly no one could understand him. He finally calmed down and described the past two hours as an 'out of dog experience.' Her

brother tried to find some more of the black
beverage the next day but he found most humans
guarded this liquid carefully and did not leave their
cups around for dogs to drink. Peso was never the
same after that and he always kept an eye out for a
forgetful tourist leaving their morning cup of hot
'liquido' somewhere. He wanted to have that 'out
of dog experience' again.

Centavo wondered if this excited dog had just
finished drinking some of the morning drink before
coming outside. Jackson finally came over to sniff
Centavo and she was able to determine he was a
male dog. His hair was so long he looked like a
cotton ball with legs with a sharp pointed nose and
mouth. He continued his hyper behavior and
would come back to Centavo after circling the
grass area a few times in order to give her another
sniff. Centavo realized this dog from 'Excite Ville'
also lived with her new owners and she would have
to learn how to be around another 'perro' from
another country. Centavo knew she needed to
make a lot of adjustments and 'hyper dog' would
just be one of them.

Jackson in a rare quiet moment getting his back rubbed

Soon Jackson got tired of running around in circles and began a more thorough investigation of Centavo. While this 'getting to know each other' phase between the two dogs was going on, Pam and Scott were sitting in the morning sun just inside the sliding glass doors drinking the black, hot drink humans like when they first get up in the morning. They were talking in their language and the only words understood by Centavo were 'doctor' and 'dog.' El doctor and many other Mexican words are the same in the language of the tourists and Centavo realized she could learn this language quickly and become a bilingual dog in no time.

In the afternoon Scott called Centavo to the door.
He kept saying,

"Come here girl," and Centavo could tell by the
tone of his voice he was talking to her. She was
still outside enjoying the grass and all the different
plants never seen in a desert environment. He
seemed to want her to come into the room where
the cars were resting and to get into the backseat
again. Centavo was a little concerned that she may
have done something wrong and they were going to
drive her all the way back to Mexico and leave her
at the beach again.

Centavo liked riding in the car and soon her fears
went away. The car stopped in the town down the
hill in front of a nice building with stone on the
walls and a sign above the door that spelled
VETERINARIAN. Centavo had heard of people
who ate only vegetables but they were called
vegetarians. This sign was different and she knew
this was a new word for her to learn.

Scott attached the leather string to Centavo's collar
and they both walked into the building. Several
humans were inside with dogs and 'gatos' in cages.
Not many gatos lived in San Felipe and the few
seen by Centavo were in windows of homes, and
not on the streets or along the waterfront. All the

dogs and gatos came in many different colors and sizes.

When Centavo tried to communicate with the dogs, they kept saying they did not understand her. Only one dog seemed to know a few words in Spanish because his owners were originally from Mexico and still spoke Espanol at home. They were trying to have their kids become integrated into the language of Estados Unidos so they spoke mostly the tourist language outside the 'casa'. The partially bi lingual dog told Centavo the language they spoke was called English but the people called themselves American. Why they did not call the language American was beyond the knowledge of the dog, whose name was Pepe. He also told Centavo that 'gatos' were called cats. Now she could add another word to her vocabulary. Centavo now knew the name of the tourist language and she was even more determined to learn it.

After a short wait a woman in a white coat came into the room where all the humans and their dogs and cats were waiting. She motioned for Scott to follow her. Centavo and Scott went into a room with a tall table made of a shiny material that had a paper cover in the middle. Scott pick up Centavo and placed her on the table and kept petting while saying,

"Everything is fine."

The woman in the white coat had some tubes coming out of her ears and on the end of the tubes was a shiny metal object that the woman kept placing all over Centavo's body. The woman in white seemed to be listening for something. She told Scott,

"Since this dog came from Mexico, we should check her stomach to see if everything is ok in that area. Dogs, like humans, pick up microbes and some are not healthy for the animals."

The woman gave Centavo a poke with a sharp pin object, which hurt a little bit. Soon she felt sleepy and had to lie down on the table in the room. Centavo did not know how long she was asleep but when she awoke she was back at the house with Pam and Scott and the bouncing fur ball in the next room.

"We had to do a minor surgery on her," Scott told Pam. "They found fish netting in her stomach and we will have to give her medicine for worms. She is fine now and will have to rest for a few days until we can remove the stitches and let her run around in the back yard. Winter is coming so she will have to get used to being inside for a few months anyway; it should be ok to keep her inside. Also, have you been thinking of a name for her?"

Just as he asked the question Scott reached back onto the counter in the kitchen and accidently knocked some coins onto the floor.

"Wow!" he said. "This must be a sign. We may have been given a divine intervention as to what her name should be. The choice could be quarter, dime, nickel or penny. The first three are pretty stupid names for a dog but Penny might work. What do you think Pam?"

"Penny is a cute name," said Pam. "Penny it is."

This is how Centavo, a dog from Mexico, became Penny, a dog from America.

Chapter 7

Adjusting to a Dog's Life in America

When the Pam and Scott started calling Centavo by the new name Penny, she was able to adjust to the change easily. After all they were feeding her twice a day and she had a bed inside an American house with a warm covering all over the floor. Centavo started to answer to her new name and came to the conclusion,

"The Anderson's could have called me Loco Weed and I would have responded."

Accepting change was not difficult as long as the food, petting and walks on the leather string continued to happen. Penny found out the last name of Pam and Scott by reading the junk mail left around on the couch. She would see their first names with Anderson after it and because Penny was so smart she was able to sound out the word and store it in her English vocabulary.

The medication to clean out any microbes in her system lasted for five days and after the stitches were pulled out from the minor surgery, Penny started to feel like her old self again. As she was recovering she also noticed a cat in the house. It came in the house through a funny small door cut into the bottom of the big door, leading to the room where the cars rested. This cat was also a fur ball like Jackson and when she saw Penny for the first time she hissed and let Penny know not to mess with her. Penny basically ignored the cat whose name turned out to be Zoe.

Zoe the cat looking out at the winter snow.

"Where do humans get these names for their animals?" thought Penny.

"Why can't they name them something based on what they do? Meow would be a good name for a cat."

Jackson told Penny the name of the cat and Penny was able to understand the words, 'name' and 'cat' so she was able to understand 'hyper dog' and what he was trying to say to her. Penny figured she better learn English because she would never get Jackson to sit long enough to teach him Spanish. Since they shared the same dinnertime and the same food, as well as being let out of the house to water the plants and 'poop', Penny and Jackson spent a lot of time together. Penny did not get too excited, except when Jackson started barking when someone came to the house and rang the doorbell.

"That's our job." Jackson told Penny. "Bark when someone approaches the house and the Anderson's will think we are earning our keep by warning them that other humans are approaching."

Penny followed Jackson's lead on this one and barked right along with Jackson, the puffball. She did not want the Anderson's to think she was not earning her keep and send her back to the fishing village in Mexico. She was beginning to love the life in America and would do anything to stay.

Jackson learned a trick from Penny after she had been in the house for only two weeks. After Scott or Pam did any work with food in the kitchen, Penny would sniff around the floor and eat any bits of eatable material that fell to the ground. This was a skill she had learned on the streets of San Felipe as she patrolled the hotels and restaurants where humans stayed or ate their meals. Food always fell to the ground and the ants never had a chance because a street dog would be there first to eat and clean up anything left behind. Now Penny had a clean kitchen floor from which to hunt for food crumbs and Jackson saw the positive benefits of such a skill.

What Jackson did, which Penny could not do because of her short height, was to lick the plates in the dishwasher clean when they were placed in the racks. After the door to the machine was closed it was too late for any special snacks or licks because the hot water and soap in the machine would clean any food from the plates and Jackson would have to wait until another load of dirty dishes arrived after a meal.

After a month of living in Flagstaff, the weather or 'clima' began to get very cold. One morning Penny woke up and could see the grass area where she scratched her back, covered with a white substance. The chairs and top of the big round bath tank, placed outside near the grass were also coated with the white stuff. Scott called the tank a 'hot tub' and occasionally both the Anderson's would put on fancy underwear and get into the big tub at night. Traje de bano or bathing suits were also worn on the beaches in Mexico so Penny knew what they were. They did this mostly when the moon was full and they would drink some kind of red stuff in a glass and talk for an hour or so. Sometimes other human friends would come over and also get into the tub with them and have long talks about a subject called 'politics.' Penny could not understand the importance of who was in power in the government. All she was concerned about was being a good guard dog with Jackson and eating two meals a day.

Scott woke up and opened the sliding door to the back yard, just like he did every morning in order to let Penny and Jackson out. He told Penny,

"This stuff is called snow, Penny. It is cold so don't stay out too long."

By now Jackson was already running around and rolling in the white substance called snow and soon his long fur was covered in the stuff. Penny came outside and also tried to roll in the cold white snow. Because she had a warm coat of fur as well, she enjoyed playing in the powder until her feet became numb. She relieved herself as usual and returned to her morning breakfast Scott had ready for her in the house. She had to be dried off with a towel before entering and it felt good to be dry again. The snow was fun for a while but there was nothing like a warm house and fire blazing in the living room fireplace. Penny preferred the warmth instead of the cold. She thought it had something to do with where she was born. Winters in her village only dropped to the freezing levels of temperature one or two nights in January and most of the day temperatures were in the 60s.

During the week Pam and Scott were gone because they worked in Flagstaff. Penny was not sure what they did but she knew Pam stayed at her work for long hours in the evening while Scott was able to drive home and let her and Jackson outside for a 'poop' break. The cat named Zoe seemed to be on her own and she went into the house from the car room whenever she wanted to. The room was called a garage and the same word in Spanish was 'garaje' so remembering that word in her new vocabulary list was easy.

Two days a week the Anderson's did not leave for work. They would get up a little later, eat breakfast or 'desayuno' and sometimes ride a bicycle that went nowhere. They called it exercise and Penny thought that this is what humans did instead of running around in the back yard and rolling in the grass or snow. If the 'clima' or weather became warm, Jackson and Penny would get to go on walks around streets where other houses and humans lived. Penny loved this the most and she could hear other dogs barking when they went by.

"Why do you get to go on walks?' They would bark. "I want to go too."

Both dogs were attached to the leather string called a leash and by now Penny knew that when the leash was brought out, she was going somewhere.

Penny, because she was born in warm Mexico, preferred the sunshine coming through the windows in the winter.

Chapter 8

Spring and Summer

After a few months of snow and cold, the weather began to change again. The sun seemed to stay out longer and the days were a little warmer. Some of the trees in town produced flowers on them and slowly the grip of winter began to loosen on the town of Flagstaff. Penny was content in her role as guard dog with Jackson, barking when humans arrived at the door. She also loved to be rubbed by friends who visited the Anderson family, especially the grown daughters of the Scott and Pam when they arrived for a visit. They really loved petting her and they also made comments about how Penny looked.

"She does look like one of the dogs the Queen of England owns."

"Some day I am going to find out who this Queen is," thought Penny.

Peggy was the name of one of the daughters who lived in the city Pam and Scott drove through when coming back from Mexico with Penny. The city was called Phoenix. She visited a lot and she was a lot of fun to be around. The other two daughters must have lived further away because their visits were not as often. Most of the time the arrival of the daughters, Joan and Sally, came in the warm period called 'verano' or summer. When the weather warmed up, walks occurred more often and both Penny and Jackson could stay out in the back yard all day when Pam and Scott were at work.

Penny was starting to forget her previous life in Mexico. She remembered her mother and sometimes wished she could see her again, but she did not miss the tough life she had lived on the streets. She used to have dreams of her life back in Mexico but slowly the dreams happened less and less and they were replaced with the life she lived now.

Being fed twice a day, petted and brushed regularly by her owners and going on walks rounded out her life style at the moment. Occasionally Scott and Pam took her and Jackson on road trips. They would have to travel in cages so they would be safe from rolling around in the car. These journeys allowed Penny to see more of this country called the United States and be able to bark to other dogs owned by humans. Penny could bark in English quite well now and whenever she came across another dog, also brought to America from Mexico, they would communicate in Spanish asking each other,

"Where did you come from?" or, "How long have you lived in America now? Have you ever gone back for a visit?

All these questions and speaking in Spanish again made Penny a little homesick for some of her dog friends. Most of the dogs she met from Mexico also came from the streets and lived a tough life of survival. They also did not want to go back to their old life of having to look for food every day and barely getting by. Living with a family was a good life and living with a family in the United States was even better.

Fourteen dog years passed, two years in human time, and the Anderson's wanted to go on another trip. Pam came into the room and asked Penny in Spanish.

"Queres visitar Mexico Penny?"

Pam would occasionally speak to her in Spanish in order to practice the language and hopefully allow Penny to remain a bilingual dog. Scott was also learning Spanish and he too would drop a phrase or two on Penny such as,

"Vaya a pasear Penny" or Let's go for a walk.

When Pam asked Penny if she wanted to visit Mexico, all kinds of dog emotions came up for her. Pam did say 'visit' so Penny knew she would be coming back to Flagstaff. She wondered if they meant a trip to her old fishing village, San Felipe. Penny thought she would like to see her friends again but at the same time she had been gone for two human years, almost as long as she lived in Mexico before coming to the United States. She was a different dog now and even though she still barked Spanish, she wondered how her family and friends would feel towards her.

After Jackson found out the Anderson's were going to Mexico, he became excited. It did not take much to get Jackson excited anyway but the thought of visiting the country where Penny came from was really a big deal to him.

"What's it like in Mexico? Are thetr any female dogs who would like to go for a walk on a beach with me? Can they bark English? What is the food like? Will we be safe?"

The endless questions poured from Jackson. Because he had never been out of the country, all the news about Mexico came from Penny.

"I had several girl friends who are your height and would go on a walk along the beach with you. All you have to do is feed them a meal. Some of them bark a little English. The Mexican food is spicy compared to the 'comida' in Flagstaff. We are probably safer in my hometown than in most cities across America. Stop watching all those false news shows about Mexico, Jackson."

Jackson practiced barking in Spanish with Penny for the next few weeks. He wanted to make an impression on the girl dogs in Mexico. He was going to say he was a relative of Lassie, hoping they would know about the dog television star. After all he looked like Lassie only shorter. Being a type of miniature collie did not stop Jackson from having a grandiose image of himself. He was loveable and he was going to strut his stuff in Mexico.

Chapter 9

Return to Mexico

The day of the trip finally arrived. It was Spring break and by now Penny figured out both Pam and Scott worked in education because all their holidays were at the same time all the school kids were out of school. Penny reasoned that Pam must work with smaller children because she was so tired at the end of the day and young kids tend to tire out humans more than older ones. Scott seemed to have a more flexible schedule and even though he was tired and needed a glass of the red drink humans sometimes drank at the end of the day, he did not seem as exhausted as Pam. Pam needed a trip to Mexico to unwind and speak the language again while Scott, who was learning the language, wanted the opportunity to practice as much as he could. He even practiced with Penny more since deciding on a return visit to Mexico.

"Quere desayuno Penny?" or "Venga aqui Penny. Vamos a Mercado ahora."

Asking if I wanted breakfast was a silly question thought Penny. Of coarse I want breakfast.

'Come here' was something she always did, and 'let's go to the market' was a trip Penny loved to do with Scott. Penny liked it when the Anderson's practiced their Spanish with her. Even though she could not bark back the correct word when they made a mistake, she understood what they said. She was also getting excited about the trip and a little uneasy at the same time. Who would still be living near the Playa? Would her mother still remember her? Was Pero still alive? What would it be like after being gone for two years and living the life of a dog from the United States?

Saturday morning arrived and Scott loaded the cages used to transport Penny and Jackson into the large car with all the room. They both had nice beds in the containers and travel was always fun because, when they stopped for food and poop breaks, Penny got to see and talk to other dogs who happened to be at the same rest stop. After they were all loaded, they started down the hill towards Phoenix. This big city, only two hours drive from Flagstaff, was always warmer than Flagstaff. Because they had to go uphill to reach Flagstaff, higher elevation had something to do with the cooler weather and snow during the winter.

Penny remembered the small town with the funny objects in it. The flying saucer was still in place and the large green object with the long neck still stood outside the gas station with all the tourist items for sale in the store behind the pumps. Jackson barked at the metal animal with the long neck but soon realized it was not alive because it never moved. About an hour later Scott pulled into another place Penny remembered. This was where Penny witnessed, for the first time, another human cleaning up dog poop in a plastic bag and putting it into the basura. Penny was used to this behavior by now and now knew why she never saw dog droppings on any of the vacations she took with the Anderson's. America was a 'poop free' nation.

Scott went into the store, which had undergone some changes since the last time they traveled through two years ago. He bought the same drink made from the dates grown in the forest of palm trees behind the store. The new building looked nothing like the old one. It now sold Quiznos sandwiches and many more tourist items. The old gas station across the street was closed and the new one next to the store was busy putting fuel into the many cars stopping at the Dateland rest stop. Penny and Jackson were taken to the grass area near the palm trees to relieve themselves and Scott cleaned up afterwards. America really seemed to be concerned about keeping clean and dog poop had no place in the master plan.

After the break and both dogs and humans were back in the car, Scott told Pam about the shake he was drinking.

"There are no more big chunks in the shake. The dates are now chopped up into small pieces and go through the straw easily. I really miss the big chunks and getting them caught in the straw. Now I have nothing to do while drinking and driving. I liked having to blow out the big chunks in the straw and eating them later when the drink was done."

"Humans are funny," thought Penny.

When Pam and Scott made her life easier she did not complain. She never wanted to go looking in trashcans for food again. She was not upset because she did not have to sleep on the cold beach in the winter without a roof over her head. Not having large chunks of fruit in your shake because the dates were now small and could easily be sucked up into the straw seemed liked such a small change to overcome compared to the life of a street dog in Mexico.

"If I were a human," thought Penny, "I would appreciate all the things that made my life easier."

Soon the town of Yuma appeared on the drive to Mexico. Scott had a choice as to which border to cross. He could drive to the San Luis border about thirty miles from Yuma or the new Mexicali/Calexico border fifty miles towards San Diego. The San Luis border had a fast toll road, which allowed the cars to speed towards Mexicali and connect to highway 5. The new border went through the city of Mexicali and continued on a back road taking the driver through the wealthy part of the city.

Penny had never seen the nice part of Mexicali where all the big houses were located and fancy stores selling clothing and Toyota cars. When Scott chose to go this way into Mexico Penny thought she was still in the United States. Only the occasional taco stands along the street reminded her they were back in Mexico again.

After crossing the border Scott let both Penny and Jackson sit in the back seat so they could look out the windows on the drive through Mexico. Jackson was excited to be in a foreign country and had a difficult time remaining seated.

"Mira," he said to Penny in Spanish. "Look at all the food stands along the sidewalks. Everything is so colorful here and people are everywhere. This is an exciting place. I have one question Penny. Where are all the dogs you said were living on the streets in Mexico?"

Jackson was right. There were few street dogs in Mexicali at the moment. When Penny came through the town two years before there were many more stray dogs living on the streets, looking for food and sleeping outside. Now the dog population was much lower. What happened?

On the drive towards San Felipe, Penny kept thinking about all the changes she was seeing. The road seemed almost new without all the holes in the pavement. Before she remembered seeing the bodies of dogs, hit by cars while they were trying to cross the road. She heard Pam telling Scott she had counted six dead dogs the last time they came through Mexico and now she could not find one body. Scott answered,

"Maybe only the smart dogs are left. Remember the expression we heard when we were here the last time. There are no dumb dogs in Mexico. Maybe that is why there are no dead dogs along the side of the road anymore."

Pam was happy to not see any dead animals on the drive south. She was sensitive to the cruelty to animals and that was one of the main reasons they decided to adopt Penny and take her back to Flagstaff with them. Penny was also sensitive to the cruelty to her species, which in her case was a dog She was also happy the road to her old home was clear of any dead bodies of her brothers and sisters. Something had changed in Mexico but Penny still did not know yet what it was.

The car arrived in San Felipe and the Anderson's checked into a hotel right on the beach near the Malecon or boardwalk near the water. Jackson was going crazy. He had never seen an ocean before. The white sand on the beach or 'playa' was filled with small fishing boats called 'pangas' and fishermen mending their nets in the warm sun. Scott had to put Jackson and Penny on a leash while they unpacked the car. Both dogs were happy to be at the end of the trip and they wanted to go to the sandy playa and run up and down the edge of the water. As soon as the suitcases and cages were put into the room, Pam took Penny and Scott took Jackson and led them to the shore near the hotel. When they got to the water both dogs were taken off their leashes and they both ran along the water as fast as they could.

Jackson could run much faster than Penny so he kept running ahead and coming back for her. They both did not go too far from the Scott and Pam because they always stayed near their owners, wherever they went. Jackson kept asking Penny,

"Where are all the girl dogs? I though you said there many dogs who lived on the beach and the boardwalk. I have been practicing my Spanish and I want to impress the pretty girl dogs of Mexico with my bilingual barking."

Penny was just as confused as Jackson as to why there were no dogs walking or running along the Malecon. Where were her friends and family whom she had not seen since she left two years ago? Why were no dogs living and sleeping along the waterfront near the fishing boats? This was not what Penny expected at all and she was starting to get worried she might not find her family or see any of her friends again.

Pam and Scott caught up with Jackson and Penny and they too were asking each other why there were no more dogs living on the beach. They were both surprised at the changes that had happened in the last two years. Even though the dog situation had changed in the village, Jackson still enjoyed the run along the beach, occasionally getting wet in the warm water of the Sea of Cortez. Penny also enjoyed the run and seeing her place of birth again. This was the first time she actually enjoyed the beach and had a run with a full stomach. For the two years she lived here she never played on the beach like she was doing now. Not having to look for food all the time made a big difference. Now she was a dog from the United States on vacation so she was able to play and have fun with Jackson and her new family.

After an hour of romping on the beach, Pam and Scott took the dogs back to the hotel, dried them off and fed them. They still ate the small round dry dog food but this time Scott had gone to a taco vendor and purchased some meat and put it on top of the American dog food. Penny told Jackson,

"This meat is what I used to eat when people threw away food in the trash cans. It may be a little spicy for you so drink water if it is too hot."

Jackson liked the spicy meat. He told Penny,

"Arf, I really like it here. The food is tasty and the beach and water are a great play area for dogs to run and have fun."

Penny just listened to Jackson and did not say much. She knew what the life in Mexico was really like, especially if you did not have an owner to take care of you. Even the dogs owned by Mexican families did not have the same privileges she and Jackson had living with the Anderson family in Flagstaff. A Mexican dog may be fed by their owner each day but most of them slept outside on the porch during the cold winter nights. Their job was to bark and warn their owners of anyone approaching the house who did not live there. Life was not easy for most dogs from Mexico, especially those who lived like Penny, two years ago.

The trip to San Felipe from Flagstaff was long and both dogs went to sleep in their cages early. Scott and Pam stayed up and typed on the portable boxes they carried with them, telling their friends they were safe in Mexico. During the night Penny had many dreams. She dreamed about her mother, Cha Cha and Pero. Her favorite brother, Peso, was also in her dreams and they all told her how happy they were she had found a good home. They hoped they would see her again and told her there had been many changes since she left. They would tell her about the changes when they saw her again.

Chapter 10

Where Have All the Stray Dogs Gone?

Penny woke up early, just as the sun was rising out of the Sea of Cortez. She had missed seeing this most wonderful sight. A large ball of orange and red coming out of the water and moving up into the sky, bringing warmth and light to the dark earth. Penny loved this memory the most. Scott must have enjoyed it as well because he got up early just to watch the sunrise from the hotel patio. Penny did a little 'dog prayer' hoping she would find out today what had happened to all the dogs on the beach.

After breakfast and a poop break for the dogs, the Anderson's brought out the leashes, indicating Jackson and Penny were going for a walk. Since the hotel was right next to the Malecon, they first walked north along the waterfront. Many food restaurants were located along the water because tourists and Mexicans loved to eat and watch the sea at the same time. The few dogs Penny saw where smaller than she was and on leases as well. The owners seemed to be either tourist or humans from the north who may have moved to Mexico. Penny knew she was not going to get any information from these yappy little dogs even though some of them could bark in Spanish. They were never street dogs and their trendy haircuts and fancy collars told Penny they had been taken care of all their lives.

All of a sudden Penny saw him. It was Pero, the wise dog her mother introduced her to when she was about to be on her own, and also the dog Penny thought might be her father. He was standing with some Mexican humans who were practicing their music near the wall on the beach. Penny knew these Mexican humans because they were on the Malecon all the time playing for the tourists and Mexican humans who came to the Playa to eat and shop. Penny got excited and pulled on her leash hoping Pam would allow her to go over to Pero and talk to him. Pam said,

"Scott, Penny wants to go over to that short dog with those men. She seems to know him and is tugging on the lease really hard in order to have me walk her over there. I think we should let her visit him for a while."

"Okay" said Scott. "I'll sit on the wall with Jackson. He seems to be interested in all the female dogs walking by anyway. Penny does not need Jackson to interfere with her visit."

Penny was so excited to see Pero. He at first did not recognize her but as soon as she started to bark at him he answered,

"Centavo! Where have you been? It has been years since I last saw you. So much has happened. When you left, your brother, Peso saw you get into a car with some tourist humans. We thought you might have been adopted and hoped you were safe. What a good surprise to see you again."

Penny was so excited to see Pero again as well. She knew she only had a short time to visit and she had so many questions.

"Pero, have you seen any of my family? I am here on a short visit and I want to see them. Where are all the street dogs and why is the Playa empty from all the dogs that used to live here? I am so happy to see you and at the same time a little concerned about all the changes I have seen in town."

For the next few minutes Pero quickly gave the answers to all of Penny's questions. She told him her name was changed from Centavo to Penny so he now barked to her using the name Penny. Pero told Penny both her brothers were adopted by the

humans from north of the border. One of them lived in one of the communities near San Felipe

while Peso moved to a land called Colorado. Her
mother, Cha Cha, died last year while having
another litter of puppies. Pero thought she just
wore out from having so many babies and her body
could not take it anymore.

Pero also told Penny about the humans from the
north who now lived in town and decided to help
with the overpopulation of dogs on the streets and
Playa. The change came soon after Penny left.
Every month a few dogs were collected by the
humans from the north and taken to a place where
they were fed and cleaned up. Each dog was given
a shot to put them asleep and when they woke up,
they all had a few stitches in their body. After that
two things happened. Either the dog was adopted
by a family or released back on the street. The
ones on the street were fine except for one main
difference. None of the girl dogs had puppies
again. Cha Cha was not picked up in time and
when she had her last litter of puppies, the strain on
her body proved to be too much and she died. Her
puppies were taken by the gringo humans from the
houses near San Felipe and given homes. They
were grown now and sometimes Pero would see
them coming into town with their new owners.

They were happy to have food given to them and
not have to live a life of eating fish, beef and other
food thrown into 'basuras' near the beach.

Pero used the word 'gringo' to describe the non-Mexican humans who now lived in or near the town. Pero said the changes were for the better because many of the dogs from the street now had a home to live in and protect. Many of the older dogs, not adopted, died of old age and the humans gave them a good burial in the desert so the wild animals would not eat them. The female dogs did not have litters of puppies any more and eventually all the dogs without owners were gone.

Pero told Penny he was adopted by a Mexican man named Juan. Juan had two important jobs in the area. He played music for the tourists with his friends and he drove a water truck used to fill the water cisterns for the many gringo homes in a development north of town. Juan spoke good English and he took Pero with him so he had a companion while he delivered water. It was also Pero's job to help Juan watch out for snakes, especially rattlesnakes. The sidewinder rattlesnakes liked to hang out near the tanks where the water was stored for the houses.

Pero wanted to describe the beautiful homes these gringos lived in but time was running out for their visit. Penny said she was happy for Pero and his new home. She told him her new home was wonderful except the 'clima' or weather was cold in the winter. Penny was born in a warm climate and she never got used to the cold in Flagstaff. She tried to describe snow to Pero but all she could compare it to was wet cold sand on the Playa. She was sad about her mother and happy for her brothers who found new homes.

Pero said he would tell all her old friends that Centavo, who is now Penny, had come for a visit to the beach and let them know her life in Flagstaff was good. He saw many of the old pack of dogs when they came to town with their new owners. When Pero was not delivering water with Juan, he was on the Malecon with the band while they played music for the visitors who came for food and shopping.

Penny was overwhelmed with all the news she had just received from Pero. She had one last question for him before she left with Pam to rejoin Scott and Jackson.

"Are you my father?" Penny always wanted to know the answer to this question but never asked Pero when she lived in Mexico.

"I might be," said Pero. Your mother and I became a couple for a while before you were born. I know we look a lot alike, so it is possible I am your father."

"I am glad you may be my father," said Penny. "I always felt you were and now I know it could be true. Thank you papa Pero for all you did for me when I was growing up."

"De nada," barked Pero. "I always knew you were special and good things would happen to you in life. Vaya con dios."

"Pero," said Penny. "Did you know dogs are related to God in English?"

"No." said Pero. "What do you mean?"

"Dog spelled backwards is God or Dios in their language. Isn't that interesting?"

"Perro spelled backwards is 'Orrep'," said Pero. "It has no meaning. I think I am starting to like English a little more. I always felt dogs were put on this earth as a connection between the animal world and the human world. Humans could learn a lot from us about the world of animals. Goodbye for now, Penny."

Penny and Pam rejoined Scott and Jackson on the Malecon. Jackson continued to bark his Spanish phrases to the girl dogs walking by with their

owners in the hopes they would stop and bark to
him as well.

"Hola chica. Que pasa con usted?"

Many of the girl dogs would glance at him but only
a few of them would answer.

"Where are you from?" they asked. "Where did
you get that accent?"

Jackson did not understand everything they said
and by the time he was able to put together another
sentence in Spanish, the girl dogs were gone with
their owners. Jackson did stand out in the Mexican
dog world. No one had seen a miniature collie
before and the black and white TV show, called
'Lassie', was no longer popular. Even if Jackson
were able to tell the girl dogs he was a cousin of
Lassie, they would not know what he was talking
about.

Scott and Pam decided to give the dogs a treat.
One of the restaurants called the Taco Factory was
located right on the Malecon. Scott and Pam's first
meal was eaten at this location on their first visit
two years ago. The restaurant was also located
near the spot where they first discovered Penny and
began asking if anyone owned her.

For lunch the Anderson family ate at one of the tables outside on the sidewalk and they ordered a special side dish of chicken and shrimp for Jackson and Penny. Jackson had never eaten shrimp before but it was 'love at first bite.'

"This pink food is really tasty." Jackson told Penny.

"I know," answered Penny. "I used to eat it all the time when tourist threw away what they could not eat. They even have a party down here every year called the Shrimp Festival and that is when the street dogs get plenty of scraps from the cans. People eat the shrimp which is prepared in many different ways and the dogs get to enjoy all the leftovers"

Jackson was in beach dog heaven. He did not know why Penny left this town. Pretty girl dogs could be seen walking by with their owners and the food was especially good. Jackson liked the spicy flavors and he also enjoyed learning and speaking the language when he had a chance.

Penny did not say anything to Jackson as to why she felt okay about leaving Mexico. He would never know how difficult it was for dogs living on

the streets to survive. Jackson was born into a
family
and he would never know the hardships Penny and
other dogs like her went through. Penny was
lucky. It was natural for her and other dogs from
the Malecon to want a better life. They were just
like dogs born in the U.S. and they could do the
same jobs of being a companion to gringos or
guarding their houses. Change was coming to
Mexico. A few of the Americans living in San
Felipe had started something affecting the lives of
the humans and the street dogs forever.

The Anderson's spent several more days in the
hotel, enjoying the slower, relaxed pace of life in
Mexico. Scott continued using the small box that
he carried around with him to send messages to his
friends back in America. Penny noticed many
humans had these devices called computers.
When she went on walks in Flagstaff there were
even special places where humans drank the
morning dark liquid called coffee and typed on the
computers for hours.

A place called Starbucks was a popular coffee
house and Pam often visited one on weekends to
get one of the fancy drinks with funny names. One
even came in a Mexican size called grande. When
Penny went with her she was sometimes given a
taste of the cake treat Pam purchased to eat with the

coffee. Penny thought her brother Peso, who now
lived in Colorado, would love this place and hoped
we would get a chance to drink some coffee again.
He was always trying to get more of the drink since
his first 'out of dog experience' back in San Felipe.

During the short visit to San Felipe, Penny crossed
paths with one more dog she knew from the life on
the street. She was the daughter of Cha Cha
only younger than Penny so she was a half sister.
She was taller than Penny becausethe big brown
dog who used to live near the beach was her father.
Her name was Blanca because she was almost all
white. She had been picked up by the gringos more
than a year ago and given the operation so she
could not have puppies. Blanca was adopted by a
human after the operation and went to live with
five other dogs.

Blanca, the half-sister to Centavo

Blanca just happened to be in town, shopping for dog food with her owner when she met Penny. She told Penny about her new life and said it was almost like living on the streets because she lived with so many other dogs. The difference was she had food to eat everyday and she slept on a soft mat on the porch every night with her new dog family. She also lived in a nice house in a community north of the town. Many street dogs from the beach also lived in the community and she saw them all the time taking walks with their new owners.

Another piece of information about humans was given to Penny. Blanca said the houses where she lived received the energy to turn on the lights and run the fans to cool the house with energy from the sun. They did not have the 'electricidad' or electricity coming from wires like the houses in town. These special black walls used to collect the sun's rays somehow changed sunshine into the energy needed to light the house and keep it cool. Since the sun came out almost every day in the desert, the dark walls used to collect the sun were working all the time.

Penny had never heard of such a thing. She knew the sun was in the sky a lot where she lived in the state of Arizona but she had never seen any black walls used to change the sun into energy on any house.

"Maybe the people in Mexico are more advanced than those living in other areas where the sun shines a lot," said Penny. "Mexico might be doing something and making it work before the Estados Unidos figured out it was a good thing to change the sun into energy."

Penny said good-by to Blanca and wished her well. Penny was glad so many changes had come to the dogs in San Felipe. She hoped other dogs on the streets in other Mexican towns would also have a chance to be adopted by someone and stop having

to search for food everyday in cans in order to
survive.

Chapter 11

Going Home

The last day in San Felipe arrived and both Pam and Scott seemed rested and ready to finish out the school year with renewed spirits. Jackson had a wonderful time playing on the beach with Penny and occasionally taking a dip into the warm waters of the Sea of Cortez. This trip for Penny had been one of closure and tying up loose ends in her life. She confirmed in her mind Pero was her father and found out all her friends and family members were safe in their new homes. She accepted the fact her mother was now in a peaceful place. She also played on the beach for the first time in her life, running up and down the sand and picking up sticks, thrown by Scott. She had to compete with Jackson, who ran much faster than she did, in getting the sticks. But she did not care if she was the first to fetch the stick; she was just having fun in her old home. She only hoped the Anderson's would return to San Felipe again so she could catch up on the news from her father, Pero.

The drive to the border took a little more than two hours, passing through mountains that came down to the sea and small Mexican Campos built on the

waters of the Colorado River. Penny heard Scott
say to Pam that many years ago the waters of the
mighty Colorado River used to cover large areas of
the flat, sandy delta area south of Mexicali. Water
use for cities like Las Vegas, Phoenix, and farming
in all the states bordering the river had reduced the
amount of water making its' way into Mexico.
Now only a few small streams made the complete
journey to the Sea of Cortez. A few farming
communities were able to sustain their food
production ability, using what waters did make it
across the border. Scott always seemed to know a
lot about Mexico and anything he needed to know
he found out on his computer box he carried with
him all the time. When he did not know the answer
to a question Pam asked him, he would tell her,
"I'll just Google it."

Humans were clever in what they could do but
Penny was not jealous of them. She and Jackson
and other animals had something humans did not
seem to have. Dogs could sense when people or
other animals were angry, sad, happy or dangerous.
Penny figured human may have the ability but it
was not as developed in them as it was with other
animals. She was also content to be in a home and
protect the house for her human owners and get fed
twice a day. She loved to curl up at the feet of Pam
or Scott in the evening and feel the warmth of the

fireplace on cold winter nights. She was petted every day and loved by her new family that found her in Mexico two year ago. Penny was finally living what the humans called, 'a dog's life.'

The border crossing took a little time because the Anderson's did not have a special pass allowing them to go into a fast lane. While they waited to cross into California, Scott again asked one of the many men, who cleaned cars, to wipe the dust off his vehicle and scrub the windows. He liked having a clean automobile and using this service while waiting in line to cross into California made good sense. Pam was able to buy some Mexican purses for her daughters in the States from pretty young girls selling handmade crafts. Scott always seemed to be adventurous in his eating habits and bought some Mexican nuts in a bag. He said they were good but on the spicy side. Pam decided to pass on the nuts and instead finished the apple and banana she purchased in San Felipe. She had to eat any remaining food items or throw them away because California was strict about not allowing food from Mexico into their state.

The guard at the gate took a look at Penny and Jackson in the cages and asked if the shot papers were in order. Scott said yes but was not asked to produce the papers. The Border patrol is more concerned with people and drugs being smuggled into their country and a few dogs are not a concern to the American authorities. The passports were returned and the family was off to the next stop in Yuma.

While Pam was getting her magic coffee drink in the Starbucks store, Scott took Penny and Jackson to a park area where the plastic bag trick was used to clean up any poop. Penny still did not see this technique being used in Mexico and guessed it would be a long time before dog poop was put into trashcans in her old town. They returned to pick up Pam. The next stop was for Scott. Dateland and the shake he always drank came next on the list. The town with the flying saucer appeared out the window and Jackson barked with excitement when he saw this strange object. Soon the large city called Phoenix, with all the tall buildings, appeared through the windows with so many cars speeding by.

On this trip, Pam and Scott did something differently than the last time they returned from Mexico. Instead of going all the way to Flagstaff, they stayed the night in Phoenix at the apartment of their daughter, Peggy. Of all their children, Peggy lived the closest to Flagstaff where Pam and Scott lived. She had just become the owner of a small white dog about the size of a large dog dish. His name was Kai and he liked having Penny and Jackson stay overnight for a visit. He was so small he could jump up and into the laps of all the humans who were in the house and get more attention than Jackson. Penny liked Kai and knew they would be friends when he came up to Flagstaff for a visit. Kai already knew how to bark when someone came to the door and many times he heard someone coming before Penny or Jackson did.

After the night was spent in Phoenix with Kai and Peggy, the Anderson's were on the road again. They made one more stop at a store called Trader Joe's and purchased all the items they could not get in Flagstaff. They arrived home around 3:00 p.m. and Penny could tell the spring weather in the area had arrived. The trees were bending with the strong winds and both dogs were happy to be inside, out of the cool breezes coming from the east. This was the time of year when the neighbor's wind machine was spinning around rapidly, providing him with enough power to heat the water in his house. Scott talked about all this information after 'Googling' it and that is how Penny knew so much about wind power.

After all the food and shopping were put away and the dogs were fed, Scott turned on the fireplace to

warm up the house. Penny and Jackson lay in front
of the heat source and went to sleep. While she
was asleep Penny had another dream. She dreamed
a lot but the dreams she had about her family were
the most real. This 'sueno' had her mother visiting
her. It was so real. Penny remained on the floor
and listened to what her mother had to say to her.

"Centavo," she said. "I know you have a new name
but to me you will always be Centavo. This is a
special visit from your mother to my most special
daughter. Your have been given a great gift in life
and have escaped the cycle I lived while on earth. I
worked hard in caring for many puppies in life and
it wore me out. I died at a young age because of
the strain put on me in caring for my puppy
children. I visit Pero in dreams as well and he has
been telling me about all the changes that are
happening in Mexico. Also you are correct in
believing Pero is your father. All my children are
in homes now and the gringos are making sure no
other dogs without homes are having puppies they
cannot care for. Because homes have been found
for many dogs in San Felipe, only a few are left on
the streets. Be happy where you are and know you
are a part of the change coming to Mexico and the
world of dogs. I will visit you again in dreams and
keep watch over you in this life. You are with two

special humans who have given you a home and you need to continue to be the best dog you can in this life. Don't worry, be happy."

Penny had heard the last expression before but she remembered it in a song. She wondered if there was a radio station in 'dog heaven' and her mother borrowed the last sentence from a singer named Bobby something.

Penny awoke and continued to lay by the fireplace with Jackson. She felt a special warmth come over her and knew it must be her mother who had visited her in the dream. She knew she was home and nothing could take that away from her. She made a little dog prayer to all the other dogs and cats in the world.

"May you all find a home and be cared for in this life."

After saying the prayer, Penny rolled over and went back to sleep. Life was good and she was happy. Fin (the end)

In Memory Of
Steve Forman

Steve Forman came to the small fishing village of San Felipe in 2003. He saw the conditions of the dogs living on the street and heard the complaints of the tourists and residents from his home country. Steve could have joined in with the complaining but instead he decided to do something about it. Steve joined with a Phoenix housewife who had founded San Felipe Animal Rescue (SFAR). He became the administrator.

For the past seven or eight years Steve organized fund raising events, holding gatherings with rock bands, Diva singers, selling shoes and everything he could think of to raise money. Cash was needed each month to bring a veterinarian to spay and neuter stray animals in and around the town of San Felipe. Those who owned a pet were also welcomed to have them "fixed" for a discounted fee or in some cases for free.

When the economy in the states changed the ability of the founder to provide funding to SFAR began to fail. Steve left SFAR and started ZAPP (Zero Animal Pupulation Project) in order to continue the work of spay and neuter clinics. Steve and all the volunteers who helped make this service have changed the face of homeless dogs and cats living in the area. The number of such animals has been greatly reduced through spay and neutering as well as finding adopting parents for these animals.

In the summer of 2011, just after I moved to San Felipe and after my wife Suzanne attended the last ZAPP clinic held in town, Steve Forman suddenly died in El Centro, California. The community working with Steve was in shock. Who would carry on this great effort by this man who, through his love of animals, found families for many of the homeless pets from the streets and stopped the needless continuation of more stray dogs and cats born without shelter?

ZAPP and SFAR merged and became VIVA (Volunteers for Indigent and Vulnerable Animals) to carry on the work of saving animal lives. The first organized dinner was held in October of 2011 and plans have been made for more clinics and the fundraisers to help this great effort to continue.

It is my hope that the work of Steve, SFAR and VIVA will spread throughout Mexico and other third world countries who are also faced with this dilemma of unwanted domesticated animals. This book is a part of the fund raising effort to continue this work in the San Felipe area and hopefully throughout the countries needing this service.

In memory of the service you have done for the animal world, I salute you Steve. May your love for animals spread in this movement you joined. You will not be forgotten.

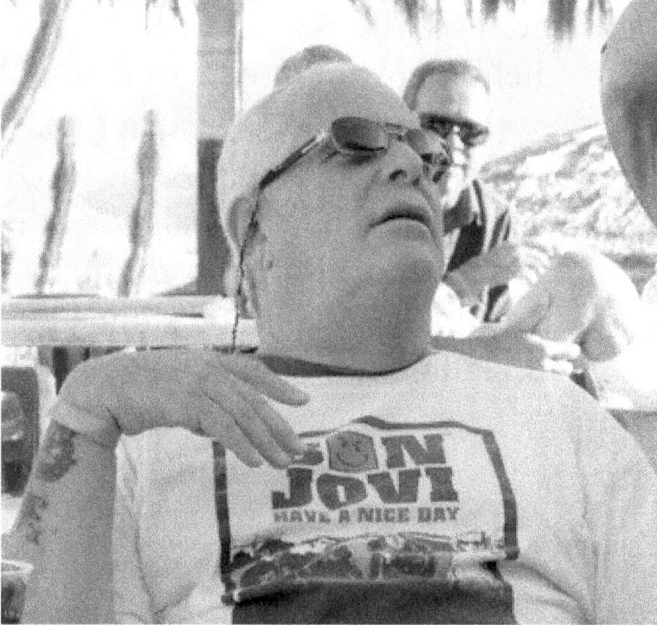

Steve relaxing during Memorial Day fundraiser, 2011

Acknowledgements

I would like to thank all the people who have adopted dogs and cats in Mexico and any other third world country around the globe. You are a part of the solution to the problem of unwanted pets found in the streets and along the roadsides everywhere. The animal's lives are difficult and usually cut short due to the lack of human care they need to survive.

If this story reaches any country where the problem of unwanted pets exist, my hope is that a program will start which provides spay and neuter services plus adoption. World health issues would be greatly improved, not to mention the lives of these unwanted animals.

The story of Centavo is based on the true story of Penny who was adopted off the streets in Mexico. The story is fiction but the situation of strays in third world countries is not. I would like to thank the pet owners who allowed me to take pictures of their dogs and cats in San Felipe. I have used their photos for the different dog and cat characters in the book. Only Penny, Jackson and the cat Zoe are themselves in the book as well as Pam and Scott

Anderson. They adopted Penny twelve years ago.

About the Author

The author lives in Baja, California near a small town call San Felipe on the Sea of Cortez. He moved there with his wife, Suzanne in 2011 after retiring from a teaching career in Special Education in 2008. He is the author of three books including **"Living Beneath the Radar; A Nine Year Journey Around the World", "Learning to Love the Peso; How to Move to Mexico and Why"** and **"Centavo; A Dog From Mexico".** He is currently working on his fourth book, **"The 60's; If You Remember it You Didn't Live it."** He continues to live in Baja, writes and lives a pace of life suitable for the creative mind. His web site is **www.JeffreyRCrimmel.com** and he can be reached through his e-mail at the site.

Author in Italy after retirement in 2008

Photos

Penny never turns down a neck rub.

Ex street dogs always look for food, even
after being adopted.

Peso begging for coffee from the tourists

San Felipe cats in a hotel downtown.

Adopted street puppy

Diccionario Para Los Palabras en El Libro
Dictionary For the Words in the Book

A

B Basura- trash
Besuqueo- petting

C Casa- house
Carne- meat
Cucaracha- cockroach
Clima- weather
Comida- food

D El doctor- doctor
Desayuno- breakfast
De nada- it's nothing, you're welcome

E electricidad- electricity
Estados Unidos- United States
Espanol- Spanish
Es su pero?- is that your dog?

F Fin- the end
G Gato- cat
Garaje- garage
Gringos- foreign tourists or residents

H   Hola chica-hi babe

I

J

K

L   Liquido- liquid
       Loco- crazy
       Leche- milk

M   Mira- look
N

O

P   Perro- dog
      Pangas- small fishing boats
      Playa- beach
      Pisos- floors

Q   Que pasa con usted?- What's happening with
you?

      Quere visitar?- Do you want to visit?
R

S   Sueno- dream
      Sombrero- large Mexican hat
      Si, perro es nuestros.- Yes the dog is ours.

T   Tiempo- time
        Traje de bano- bathing suit

U

V   Vaya a pesear- let's go for a walk
        Venga aqui- come here
        Vamos a Mercado ahora- let's go to the
        market now
        Vaya con Dios- go with God

W

X

Y

Z

www.ingramcontent.com/pod-product-compliance
Lightning Source LLC
Chambersburg PA
CBHW070528030426
42337CB00016B/2152